MW00570403

SAY IT WITH A *Cupcake*

SAY IT WITH A *Cupcake*

SUSANNAH BLAKE

with photography by
Martin Brigdale

RYLAND
PETERS
& SMALL

LONDON NEW YORK

Senior Designer Toni Kay

Commissioning Editor Julia Charles

Production Hazel Kirkman

Art Director Leslie Harrington

Publishing Director Alison Starling

Food Stylist Linda Tubby

Prop Stylist Helen Trent

Indexer Hilary Bird

Notes

• All spoon measurements are level unless otherwise specified.

• All eggs are medium unless otherwise specified.

• Ovens should be preheated to the specified temperature. If using a fan-assisted oven, cooking times should be reduced according to the manufacturer's instructions.

• When using the grated peel of lemons or limes in a recipe, try to find organic or unwaxed fruits and wash well before using.

Printed and bound in China

First published in the United States in 2009 by Ryland Peters & Small, Inc.
519 Broadway, 5th Floor
New York, NY 10012
www.rylandpeters.com

The recipes in this book were first published by Ryland Peters & Small in *Cupcakes* and *Cupcake Heaven*.

Text copyright © Susannah Blake 2009
Design and photography copyright
© Ryland Peters & Small
2007, 2008, 2009

All photography by Martin Brigdale except: Carolyn Barber page 63; David Brittain page 36; Peter Cassidy page 16; Chris Tubbs page 45; Polly Wreford pages 29 and 41.

10 9 8 7 6 5 4 3 2 1

Library of Congress Cataloging-in-Publication Data
Blake, Susannah.
Say it with a cupcake / Susannah Blake.
    p. cm.
Includes index.
ISBN 978-1-84597-914-0
 1. Cupcakes. 2. Cake decorating. I. Title.
 TX771.B565 2009
 641.8'653--dc22
                                    2009002839

Contents

Baking the perfect cupcake

The great thing about baking cupcakes is that the ingredients and equipment required are basic. The techniques are generally simple and you need only the bare kitchen essentials to be able to rustle up the most professional-looking sugary creations to give as gifts.

Although there are many variations on the classic cupcake, most cupcake mixtures are based on four basic ingredients: butter, sugar, eggs, and flour. Other ingredients such as chocolate, nuts, dried fruit, and other flavorings, such as vanilla and grated lemon zest, may then be added to the mixture to add texture and flavor. For the best results, always use unsalted butter for cupcakes. For creamed mixtures, where the butter and sugar are beaten together, the butter should be left at room temperature until soft. The most common sugar for making cupcakes is white granulated sugar, but other sugars and sweeteners (such as honey) are also used, all of which will add their own unique taste and texture. Eggs enrich cakes but also bind the ingredients together and are best used at room temperature. The eggs used in the recipes in this book are medium. Most cupcakes use self-rising flour or all-purpose flour with a little baking powder added.

Quantities are important when baking cakes and using the wrong proportions of ingredients can lead to disappointing results. So make sure you have a set of accurate cups, scales, and spoons. The easiest way to make cupcakes is to bake them in cupcake pans, which usually have six to 12 cup-shaped holes. For the prettiest effect, line them with paper liners before filling with batter. As well as standard cupcake pans, you can also find mini-cupcake ones, which some of the recipes in this book use.

Whether your oven is gas or electric is unimportant. Some ovens have hot spots, and some cook faster than others, but as you get to know your own oven, you'll know whether you need to turn the cupcake pan round partway through baking to ensure evenly browned and risen cakes, or whether you'll need to adjust the cooking time.

Decorating your cupcakes is where the fun really begins! Simple or sophisticated, plain or indulgent. From the simplest glacé icing to swirls of rich buttercream frosting—the options are endless.

Icings and frostings

Prettily colored, sugary sweet icings and frostings that you can drizzle, spoon, swirl, or pipe on top of cupcakes add a whole new dimension. Melted white or bittersweet chocolate, or a glacé icing made from confectioners' sugar and lemon juice are the simplest and are perfect for spooning or drizzling. Buttercreams, cream cheese frostings, chocolate ganaches, whipped cream, and creamy custards are more indulgent and excellent for swirling and piping.

Fondant icing, which can be bought ready-made and ready-to-roll, is perfect for making sophisticated and professional-looking cakes. White fondant icing can be splashed with a little food coloring, then kneaded to incorporate the coloring, rolled out, cut into rounds, and draped over cupcakes to give a silky smooth finish to which decorations can then be added.

Sprinkles and other decorations

Once you've frosted or iced your cupcake, you can leave it plain, but it's even more fun to add decorations. A glacé cherry or a single brightly colored candy placed in the center of the cupcake can be stunning. But there are also delightful colored sugar sprinkles that you can scatter all over frosted cakes—from sprinkles to tiny sugar shapes, such as hearts, stars, and flowers. Other decorations include sugar and rice paper flowers, gold and silver dragées, edible sparkles, and even birthday candles and firework sparklers that you can light at the table. Supermarkets and kitchen stores are full of fabulous decorations that are perfect for decorating cupcakes. Don't be afraid to let your imagination run wild!

Cupcake liners

There are many different types of pretty cupcake liner available. You can find them in supermarkets and kitchen shops and they come in a fabulous array of colors and designs. Look out for pretty pastels or bright colors, elegant floral patterns, fun prints such as soccer

balls for boys, or lovehearts for
Valentine's Day. There are shiny
metallic cases, too—gold, silver, and
other colors, or even stripes and spots.
There really is no end to the choice
out there! When giving cupcakes as
a gift, present them in cardboard or
cellophane boxes tied with ribbon
or on an attractive cake stand.

HAPPY BIRTHDAY

Birthday Surprise!

THESE DECORATE-YOUR-OWN-CUPCAKES ARE ALWAYS
A HIT AT A BIRTHDAY PARTY WITH KIDS AND GROWN-UPS
ALIKE! EVERYONE WILL ENJOY GETTING CREATIVE AND
TRYING TO PRODUCE THE MOST OUTLANDISH CUPCAKE.

Preheat the oven to 350°F.

Beat the butter and sugar in a bowl until pale and fluffy,
then beat in the eggs, one at a time. Sift the flour and
cocoa powder into the mixture and fold in.

Spoon the mixture into the paper liners and bake in the
preheated oven for about 17 minutes until risen and a skewer
inserted in the center comes out clean. Transfer to a wire
rack to cool completely.

To decorate, beat the butter until soft, then add the
confectioner's sugar and milk and beat until smooth and
creamy. Divide the frosting among three bowls. Add a few
drops of food coloring to each one and stir well to make
a vibrant lilac, yellow, and green. Spoon into serving bowls.

Arrange the cakes on a plate and put the candies and
decorations in individual bowls alongside the bowls of
frosting. Let the kids or guests decorate their own cakes.

1 stick unsalted butter,
at room temperature

½ cup granulated sugar

2 eggs

1 cup self-rising flour

1½ tablespoons unsweetened
cocoa powder

TO DECORATE

1½ sticks unsalted butter,
at room temperature

3 cups confectioners' sugar,
sifted

2 tablespoons milk

lilac, yellow, and green food
coloring

brightly colored candies,
such as jimmies, Smarties,
Skittles, Dots, and gumdrops

sprinkles, sugar flowers, and
edible colored balls

*a 12-cup cupcake pan,
lined with paper liners*

MAKES 12

1 stick butter,
at room temperature

½ cup granulated sugar

2 eggs

¾ cup self-rising flour

1 teaspoon vanilla extract

2 tablespoons full-fat milk

TO DECORATE

6 red or pink hard candies

1¼ cups confectioners' sugar,
sifted

1 egg white

lilac food coloring

edible sparkles and edible
silver balls

*a 12-cup cupcake pan,
lined with paper liners*

MAKES 12

DELIGHTFULLY GIRLY, THESE GORGEOUS, SPARKLING
CUPCAKES ARE JUST PERFECT TO BAKE FOR ANY
YOUNG GIRL'S SPECIAL BIRTHDAY CELEBRATION.

Sweet Sixteen

Preheat the oven to 350°F.

Put the butter and sugar in a large bowl and beat until
pale and fluffy. Beat in the eggs, one at a time. Sift over the
flour and fold in, then fold in the vanilla extract and milk.

Spoon the mixture into the paper liners and bake in the
preheated oven for about 17 minutes until risen and a skewer
inserted in the center comes out clean. Transfer to a wire
rack to cool completely.

To decorate, leave the candies in their wrappers and tap
with a rolling pin to break into large pieces. Set aside.

To make the frosting, gradually beat the confectioners' sugar
into the egg white until smooth and creamy, then beat in
a few drops of food coloring until the desired color has
been achieved. Spread the frosting on top of the cakes. Pile
a little heap of candy "jewels" in the center of each cake and
sprinkle with edible sparkles and silver balls. Let set slightly
before serving or packing.

Twenty One Again

THESE CUTE LITTLE PEANUT BUTTER-FLAVORED CAKES
FILLED WITH A BLOB OF FRUITY JELLY ARE JUST PERFECT
FOR THE BIG KID IN ALL OF US. THEY MAKE GREAT
MINI-DESSERTS FOR A BIRTHDAY DINNER PARTY—JUST
REMEMBER TO WARN EVERYONE THAT THEY CONTAIN
PEANUTS IN CASE ANYONE IS ALLERGIC TO THEM.

Preheat the oven to 350°F.

Beat the butter, crunchy peanut butter, and sugar together
in a bowl until pale and fluffy, then beat in the eggs, one
at a time. Sift the flour into the mixture and fold in.

Spoon dollops of the mixture into the foil liners and flatten
slightly with the back of a teaspoon, making a slight indent
in the center. Drop about ½ teaspoon jelly in the center of
each indent. Top with the remaining cake mixture. Bake in
the preheated oven for about 18 minutes until risen and
golden. Transfer to a wire rack and leave to cool completely.

To decorate the cakes, put the smooth peanut butter and
mascarpone in a bowl and beat to combine, then stir in the
confectioner's sugar until smooth and creamy. Swirl the
frosting on top of the cakes and sprinkle with edible balls.
Pop a candle in the center of each cake, if using.

4 tablespoons unsalted butter,
at room temperature

¼ cup crunchy peanut butter

½ cup granulated sugar

2 eggs

1 cup self-rising flour

2 tablespoons raspberry
or strawberry jelly

TO DECORATE

3 tablespoons smooth
peanut butter

4 tablespoons mascarpone

⅛ cup confectioners' sugar,
sifted

edible gold balls

12 candles (optional)

*a 12-cup cupcake pan,
lined with foil liners*

MAKES 12

THESE GROWN-UP CUPCAKES ARE THE ULTIMATE
INDULGENCE—MOIST, CRUMBLY CAKE WITH JUICY
RASPBERRIES AND A DRIZZLE OF KIRSCH, SMOTHERED IN
CREAMY CUSTARD, AND TOPPED WITH FRESH FRUIT. THEY
MAKE A LOVELY BIRTHDAY TREAT FOR A SPECIAL FRIEND.

Best Friend's Birthday

1 stick unsalted butter,
at room temperature

½ cup granulated sugar

2 eggs

1 cup self-rising flour

1⅓ cups fresh raspberries

TO DECORATE

1 tablespoon kirsch

¼ cup heavy cream

½ cup fresh custard sauce

7 oz. raspberries and
red currants, or other
berries of your choice

*a 12-cup cupcake pan,
lined with paper liners*

MAKES 12

Preheat the oven to 350°F.

Beat the butter and sugar together in a bowl until pale
and fluffy, then beat in the eggs, one at a time. Sift the flour
into the mixture and fold in, then fold in the raspberries.

Spoon the mixture into the paper liners and bake in the
preheated oven for 18 minutes until risen and golden and
a skewer inserted in the center comes out clean. Transfer
to a wire rack to cool.

To decorate, prick each cupcake all over with a toothpick
and pour ¼ teaspoon kirsch over each one, allowing it to
soak into the cake. Whip the cream, then fold in the custard
sauce and spoon on top of the cakes. Top each cake with
raspberries and red currants, or berries of your choice.
These cupcakes are fragile so take great care when serving
or packing them.

Boyfriend's Birthday

THESE SOPHISTICATED CHOCOLATE-MOCHA CUPCAKES
MAKE THE PERFECT BIRTHDAY TREAT FOR THE MAN IN
YOUR LIFE. SERVE WITH A GOOD STRONG CUP OF COFFEE.

Preheat the oven to 350°F.

Put the chocolate in a heatproof bowl set over a pan of gently
simmering water. Do not let the bowl touch the water. Leave
until almost melted, then set aside to cool slightly.

Beat the butter and sugar together in a bowl until pale
and fluffy, then beat in the eggs, one at a time. Stir in the
melted chocolate and cocoa powder. Sift the flour into the
mixture and stir in, then stir in the coffee, followed by the
chocolate-covered coffee beans.

Spoon the mixture into the foil liners and bake in the
preheated oven for about 20 minutes until risen and a skewer
inserted in the center comes out clean. Transfer to a wire
rack to cool.

To decorate, beat the butter, confectioner's sugar, and coffee
together in a bowl until pale and fluffy. Spread the mixture
smoothly over the cakes and sprinkle with grated chocolate.

3 oz. bittersweet chocolate,
chopped

1 stick plus 2 tablespoons
unsalted butter, at room
temperature

¼ cup granulated sugar

2 eggs

2 tablespoons unsweetened
cocoa powder

¼ cup self-rising flour

2 teaspoons instant coffee,
dissolved in 1 tablespoon
boiling water

¼ cup chocolate-covered
coffee beans

TO DECORATE

7 tablespoons unsalted butter,
at room temperature

1⅜ cups confectioners' sugar,
sifted

2 teaspoons instant coffee,
dissolved in 1 tablespoon
boiling water

grated bittersweet chocolate

*a 12-cup cupcake pan,
lined with foil or paper liners*

MAKES 12

TRUE ROMANCE

Marry Me?

THESE SEDUCTIVE CHERRY-STUDDED CHOCOLATE
CUPCAKES ARE SPIKED WITH KIRSCH AND TOPPED
WITH FRESH CREAM—SIMPLY IMPOSSIBLE TO RESIST!

Preheat the oven to 350°F.

Put the chocolate in a heatproof bowl set over a pan of gently
simmering water. Do not let the bowl touch the water.
Leave until almost melted, then set aside to cool slightly.

Beat the butter and sugar together in a bowl until pale and
fluffy, then beat in the eggs, one at a time. Beat in the melted
chocolate, then stir in the almonds. Sift the flour and cocoa
powder into the mixture and fold in, followed by the kirsch
and glacé cherries.

Spoon the mixture into the paper liners and bake in the
preheated oven for 20 minutes until a skewer inserted in
the center comes out clean. Transfer to a wire rack to cool.

To decorate, put the chocolate in a heatproof bowl. Heat the
cream in a saucepan until almost at a boil, then pour over the
chocolate and leave to melt for about 5 minutes. Stir until
smooth and creamy, then stir in the kirsch and leave to cool
for about 1 hour until thick and glossy. Spread the frosting
over the cakes, top with a blob of whipped cream, a glacé
cherry, and a few chocolate shavings. Serve immediately.

3 oz. bittersweet chocolate,
chopped

1 stick unsalted butter,
at room temperature

½ cup granulated sugar

2 eggs

2 tablespoons ground almonds

1¼ cups self-rising flour

1 tablespoon unsweetened
cocoa powder

2 tablespoons kirsch

½ cup glacé cherries, halved

TO DECORATE

3½ oz. bittersweet chocolate,
finely chopped, plus extra
chocolate shavings

½ cup heavy cream

1 tablespoon kirsch

whipped cream, to top

12 glacé cherries

*a 12-cup cupcake pan,
lined with paper liners*

MAKES 12

THESE RICH, DECADENT CHOCOLATE-ORANGE CUPCAKES,
TOPPED WITH FRAGRANT ROSE PETALS, ARE THE PERFECT
CHOICE WHEN ROMANCING A PASSIONATE CHOCAHOLIC.

Love Me, Love Me Not...

2½ oz. bittersweet chocolate,
chopped

6 tablespoons unsalted butter,
at room temperature

½ cup granulated sugar

2 eggs

3 tablespoons crème fraîche
or sour cream

1 cup self-rising flour

1 tablespoon Grand Marnier

TO DECORATE

½ cup heavy cream

3½ oz. bittersweet chocolate,
finely chopped

fresh rose petals, gently
washed and patted dry

*a 12-cup cupcake pan,
lined with paper liners*

MAKES 12

Preheat the oven to 350°F.

Put the chocolate in a heatproof bowl set over a pan of
gently simmering water. Do not let the bowl touch the
water. Leave until almost melted. Remove from the heat.

Beat together the butter and sugar until pale and creamy,
then beat in the eggs, one at a time. Stir in the crème
fraîche, then sift the flour into the mixture and fold in. Stir
in the melted chocolate, followed by the Grand Marnier.

Spoon the mixture into the paper liners and bake in the
preheated oven for 18 minutes until risen and a skewer
inserted in the center comes out clean. Transfer to a wire
rack to cool.

To decorate, gently heat the cream until almost at a boil,
then pour over the chopped chocolate and leave to melt
for about 5 minutes. Stir until the chocolate has melted,
then refrigerate for 20–30 minutes. Beat until thick and
glossy, then spoon on top of the cakes. Top each cake
with a perfect rose petal to serve.

Be My Valentine

THESE DELIGHTFULLY FLIRTATIOUS CAKES FILLED WITH
A ZESTY LEMON CREAM AND FRESH RASPBERRIES ARE
GREAT FUN TO BAKE FOR VALENTINE'S DAY.

Preheat the oven to 350°F.

Beat the butter and sugar together in a bowl until pale and
fluffy, then beat in the eggs, one at a time. Sift the flour into
the mixture and fold in, then stir in the lemon peel and juice.

Spoon the mixture into the paper liners and bake in the
preheated oven for about 18 minutes until risen and golden
and a skewer inserted in the center comes out clean. Transfer
to a wire rack to cool.

To decorate, use a sharp, pointed knife to remove a deep
round from the center of each cake, about 1 inch in
diameter. Slice the rounded bit off each piece of cored-out
cake so that you are left with a flat disk. Using the mini
heart-shaped cookie cutter, cut a small heart from each disk.

Combine the crème fraîche and lemon curd in a bowl,
then fold in the raspberries. Spoon the mixture into the
hollowed-out cakes, then top with the cake hearts. Dust
with confectioners' sugar just before serving.

1 stick unsalted butter,
at room temperature

½ cup granulated sugar

2 eggs

1 cup self-rising flour

finely grated peel and freshly
squeezed juice of ½ a lemon

TO DECORATE

⅓ cup crème fraîche or
sour cream

1 tablespoon good-quality
lemon curd

⅔ cup fresh raspberries

confectioners' sugar,
for dusting

*a 12-cup cupcake pan
(with heart-shape cups
if you can find one), lined
with paper liners*

*a mini heart-shaped
cookie cutter*

MAKES 12

Happy Anniversary

1 stick unsalted butter,
at room temperature

½ cup granulated sugar

2 eggs

1 cup self-rising flour

3 pieces of stem ginger in
syrup, drained and chopped

finely grated peel of 1 lime

TO DECORATE

about 6 clear mint candies

2½ tablespoons freshly
squeezed lime juice,
plus extra as required

1⅓ cups confectioners' sugar,
sifted

blue food coloring

edible sparkles

*a 12-cup cupcake pan,
lined with foil or paper liners*

MAKES 12

THESE SPECTACULAR DIAMOND-ENCRUSTED CUPCAKES
ARE PERFECT TO TAKE TO AN ANNIVERSARY PARTY.
A SPICY GINGER SPONGE IS TOPPED WITH A TANGY LIME
ICING, MAKING THEM A SOPHISTICATED TREAT.

Preheat the oven to 350°F.

Beat the butter and sugar together in a bowl until pale and
fluffy, then beat in the eggs, one at a time. Sift the flour into
the mixture and fold in, then stir in the ginger and lime peel.

Spoon the mixture into the foil liners, then bake in the
preheated oven for about 17 minutes until risen and golden
and a skewer inserted in the center comes out clean. Transfer
to a wire rack and leave to cool completely.

To decorate, leave the mint candies in their wrappers and
tap with a rolling pin to break into pieces. Set aside.

Put the lime juice in a bowl, add the confectioners' sugar, and
stir until smooth. Add a little more lime juice as required
to make a spoonable icing. Add a couple of drops of food
coloring and stir in to achieve a pale blue color.

Spoon the icing on top of the cakes. To decorate, pile a little
heap of mint candy "diamonds" on each cake and sprinkle
with edible sparkles.

WHO WANTS TO EAT A HEAVY SLICE OF FRUIT CAKE
WHEN THEY COULD HAVE THESE DELECTABLY LIGHT
AND DELICATE VANILLA-FLAVORED CUPCAKES INSTEAD!

Wedding Day

Preheat the oven to 350°F.

Beat the butter and sugar together in a bowl until pale and
fluffy, then beat in the eggs, one at a time. Sift the flour into
the mixture and fold in. Stir in the vanilla and the milk.

Spoon the mixture into the paper liners and bake in the
preheated oven for about 18 minutes until risen and golden
and a skewer inserted in the center comes out clean. Transfer
to a wire rack to cool.

To decorate, carefully fasten a piece of lace ribbon around
each cake. Put the egg white in a large bowl, then beat in
the sugar until thick and creamy. Beat in the lemon juice
to make a thick, spoonable icing.

Spoon the icing onto the cakes, then top each one with
a flower. The icing hardens quite fast, so work quickly as
soon as you've made the icing.

Note: you can use larger or smaller muffin pans and liners
to make a variety of sizes as these look very effective when
displayed on a tiered cake stand (as shown).

1 stick unsalted butter,
at room temperature

½ cup granulated sugar

2 eggs

1 cup self-rising flour

1 teaspoon pure vanilla extract

2 tablespoons milk

TO DECORATE

white lace or organza ribbon

1 egg white

1 cup confectioners' sugar,
sifted

½ teaspoon freshly squeezed
lemon juice

white edible flower decorations

*a 12-cup cupcake pan, lined
with paper liners (see note)*

MAKES 12

SEASONAL TREATS

Happy Easter

CHILDREN LOVE THESE LITTLE CHOCOLATE NESTS
WITH PRETTY PASTEL-COLORED EGGS NESTLING INSIDE.
THEY'RE EASY TO MAKE AND KIDS WILL HAVE A GREAT
TIME HELPING YOU TO DECORATE THEM.

Preheat the oven to 350°F.

Beat the butter and sugar together in a bowl until pale
and fluffy, then beat in the eggs, one at a time. Sift the
flour and cocoa powder into the mixture and fold in,
then stir in the milk.

Spoon the mixture into the paper liners and bake in the
preheated oven for 18 minutes until risen and a skewer
inserted in the center comes out clean. Transfer to a wire
rack to cool.

To decorate, put the mascarpone, sugar, and cocoa powder
in a bowl and beat together until smooth and creamy. Put
a dollop of frosting on top of each cake.

Arrange some chocolate shavings on top of the frosting to
create 12 little bird's nests. Finish off with three sugar-coated
chocolate eggs in the center of each nest.

1 stick unsalted butter,
at room temperature

½ cup granulated sugar

2 eggs

1 cup self-rising flour

1½ tablespoons unsweetened
cocoa powder

2 tablespoons full-fat milk

TO DECORATE

⅔ cup mascarpone

⅓ cup confectioner's sugar,
sifted

1 tablespoon unsweetened
cocoa powder, sifted

semi-sweet chocolate
shavings

36 sugar-coated chocolate
eggs (about 4 oz.)

*a 12-cup cupcake pan,
lined with paper liners*

MAKES 12

Merry Christmas

THESE LIGHTLY SPICED CRANBERRY AND PEAR CUPCAKES,
TOPPED WITH A RICH BRANDY BUTTER FROSTING, MAKE
A DELICIOUS TREAT TO BAKE AND ENJOY THROUGHOUT
THE HOLIDAY SEASON.

4 tablespoons unsalted butter, at room temperature

½ cup granulated sugar

2 eggs

1 cup self-rising flour

½ teaspoon mixed spice

1 pear, peeled, cored, and finely diced

¼ cup dried cranberries

TO DECORATE

6½ tablespoons unsalted butter, at room temperature

1 cup confectioners' sugar, sifted

4 teaspoons brandy

about 36 fresh cranberries

12 small holly leaves (optional)

edible gold balls

a 12-cup cupcake pan, lined with paper liners

MAKES 12

Preheat the oven to 350°F.

Beat the butter and sugar together in a bowl until pale and fluffy, then beat in the eggs, one at a time. Sift the flour and mixed spice into the mixture and fold in, then stir in the pear and cranberries.

Spoon the mixture into the paper liners and bake in the preheated oven for about 18 minutes until risen and golden and a skewer inserted in the center comes out clean. Transfer to a wire rack to cool.

To decorate, put the butter, sugar, and brandy in a bowl and beat together until smooth and creamy. Swirl the frosting on top of the cakes, then decorate each one with two or three fresh cranberries, a holly leaf, if using, and sprinkle with edible balls.

Happy New Year

THESE STAR-STRUCK SPONGES MAKE A DELICIOUSLY LIGHT
ALTERNATIVE TO TRADITIONAL FRUIT CAKE—PERFECT
WASHED DOWN WITH A GLASS OF CELEBRATORY FIZZ.

Make the star decorations the day before you plan to make
the cakes. Roll out the fondant icing, then use the cookie
cutter to cut out 12 stars. Set aside and leave to dry overnight.

When you are ready to make the cupcakes, preheat the oven
to 350°F.

Beat the butter and sugar together in a bowl until creamy,
then gradually beat in the egg, followed by the orange peel.
Sift the flour into the mixture and fold in, then stir in the
brandy, followed by the dried fruit and glacé cherries.

Spoon the mixture into the foil liners and bake in the
preheated oven for 14 minutes until risen and golden and
a skewer inserted in the center comes out clean. Transfer
to a wire rack to cool.

To decorate, gradually beat the sugar into 2 of the egg
whites in a bowl until smooth and creamy, then beat in the
lemon juice. Spoon the mixture over the cakes and scatter
over the silver balls. Leave to firm up slightly. Place the star
decorations on top of the cakes, brush with the remaining
egg white, and sprinkle with edible sparkles.

4 tablespoons unsalted butter,
at room temperature

⅛ cup packed brown sugar

1 egg

finely grated peel of 1 orange

½ cup self-rising flour

1 tablespoon brandy

4 ready-to-eat dried figs,
chopped

3 tablespoons golden raisins

½ cup glacé cherries, halved

TO DECORATE

3½ oz. pale blue or white
ready-to-roll fondant icing

3 cups confectioner's sugar,
sifted

3 egg whites

2½ teaspoons freshly
squeezed lemon juice

edible silver balls

edible clear sparkles

a mini star-shaped cookie cutter

*a 12-cup cupcake pan,
lined with foil or paper liners*

MAKES 12

⅓ cup packed brown sugar

1⅓ cups sunflower oil

2 eggs

1 cup grated pumpkin or
butternut squash flesh

finely grated peel of 1 lemon

1 cup self-rising flour

1 teaspoon baking powder

1 teaspoon ground cinnamon

TO DECORATE

5 oz. white chocolate,
chopped

1 oz. bittersweet chocolate

*a 12-cup cupcake pan,
lined with paper liners*

parchment paper

MAKES 12

THESE SWEET, SPICY PUMPKIN CAKES, TOPPED WITH
CREAMY WHITE AND DARK CHOCOLATE COBWEBS,
ARE DEFINITELY A TREAT RATHER THAN A TRICK!

Happy Halloween

Preheat the oven to 350°F.

Put the sugar in a bowl and beat in the oil and eggs. Fold in
the pumpkin and lemon peel. Sift the flour, baking powder,
and cinnamon into the pumpkin mixture and fold it in.

Spoon the mixture into the paper liners and bake in the
preheated oven for about 18 minutes until risen and a
skewer inserted in the center comes out clean. Transfer
to a wire rack to cool.

To decorate, melt the white and bittersweet chocolates in
separate heatproof bowls set over pans of gently simmering
water. Remove them from the heat and leave to cool for
5 minutes, then spoon the white chocolate over the cakes.

Roll a square of parchment paper into a cone and secure
it with sticky tape. Spoon the melted bittersweet chocolate
into it and snip off the tip to make a piping bag. Put a
dot of chocolate in the center of each cake, then pipe three
concentric circles around the dot. Using a skewer, draw a
line from the central dot to the outside edge of the cake
and repeat seven times all the way round to create a cobweb.

Fireworks Parties

WHETHER IT'S 4TH JULY, BONFIRE NIGHT, OR BASTILLE DAY,
THESE CHOCOLATE ORANGE-FLAVORED CAKES ARE JUST
THE THING TO SERVE WHEN THE NIGHT SKY IS EXPLODING.

Preheat the oven to 350°F.

Sift the flour, cocoa powder, and baking soda into a large
bowl. Add the sugar and mix to combine. Make a well in
the center.

Combine the orange juice and peel, oil, and vinegar in
a pitcher and pour into the dry ingredients. Quickly stir
together until combined—the mixture should be quite
liquid and gooey—then spoon it into the foil liners.

Bake in the preheated oven for about 15 minutes until risen
and firm on top and a skewer inserted in the center comes
out clean. Transfer to a wire rack to cool.

To decorate, put the chocolate in a heatproof bowl. Heat
the cream in a small saucepan until almost boiling, then
pour it over the chocolate. Let melt for 5 minutes, then
stir until smooth and creamy. Leave to cool until thick and
glossy, then spread over the cakes. Sprinkle the frosted cakes
with tiny silver balls and stick a mini-sparkler in the center
of each one. Light the sparklers just before serving.

1 cup all-purpose flour

3 tablespoons unsweetened
cocoa powder

½ teaspoon baking soda

¼ cup granulated sugar

½ cup fresh orange juice

finely grated peel of 1 orange

3 tablespoons sunflower oil

1½ teaspoons distilled
white vinegar

TO DECORATE

3½ oz. bittersweet chocolate,
finely chopped

½ cup heavy cream

edible silver balls

12 mini-sparklers

*a 12-cup cupcake pan,
lined with foil or paper liners*

MAKES 12

FAMILY TIME

Baby Shower

THESE SUPER-CUTE VANILLA-FLAVORED MINI CUPCAKES,
WITH THEIR PRETTY PASTEL TOPPINGS, ARE PERFECT FOR
SHARING WITH GIRLFRIENDS AT A BABY SHOWER.

Preheat the oven to 350°F.

Beat the butter and sugar together in a bowl until pale and
fluffy, then beat in the egg, a little at a time. Sift the flour
into the mixture and fold in, then stir in the vanilla extract
and milk.

Spoon the mixture into the petits fours liners, then bake
in the preheated oven for about 15 minutes until risen
and golden and the tops spring back when gently pressed.
Transfer to a wire rack to cool.

To decorate, divide the chocolate among three heatproof
bowls and set over pans of gently simmering water. Do not
let the bowls touch the water. Leave until almost melted.
Leave to cool slightly, then stir a couple of drops of green
food coloring into one bowl and a couple of drops of pink
into another. Leave the third bowl of chocolate plain.

Spoon white chocolate over four of the cakes, pink over
another four, and green over the remaining four, then top
each one with a candy. Serve while the chocolate is still
soft, or leave to set and package up as a gift.

½ stick unsalted butter,
at room temperature

¼ cup granulated sugar

1 egg, beaten

½ cup self-rising flour

¼ teaspoon pure vanilla
extract

1 tablespoon milk

TO DECORATE

4 oz. white chocolate,
roughly chopped

green and pink food coloring

12 pastel-color candies,
such as jelly beans

*a 12-cup mini-cupcake pan
lined with petits fours liners*

MAKES 12

THESE PRETTY-AS-A-PICTURE LEMON SPONGES WITH
A CREAM CHEESE FROSTING ARE JUST RIGHT FOR SERVING
AT CHRISTENINGS OR ANY NEW BABY CELEBRATION.

New Baby!

1 stick unsalted butter,
at room temperature

½ cup granulated sugar

2 eggs

1 cup self-rising flour

1½ teaspoons finely grated
lemon peel

TO DECORATE

4 oz. cream cheese

⅓ cup confectioner'
sugar, sifted

1½ teaspoons freshly
squeezed lemon juice

pink and blue food coloring

edible silver balls

*two 12-cup mini-cupcake pans,
lined with petits fours liners*

MAKES 24

Preheat the oven to 350°F.

Beat the butter and sugar until pale and fluffy, then beat in
the eggs, one at a time. Sift the flour into the mixture and
fold in, then stir in the lemon peel.

Spoon the mixture into the petits fours liners, then bake
in the preheated oven for about 15 minutes until risen
and golden and the tops spring back when gently pressed.
Transfer to a wire rack to cool completely.

To decorate, beat the cream cheese briefly until soft.
Gradually beat in the sugar until smooth and creamy, then
stir in the lemon juice. Divide the frosting among two bowls,
add a few drops of food coloring to each one and stir well
to make pastel pink and blue. (Alternatively use the single
color of your choice.) Swirl the frosting on top of the cakes,
then sprinkle over the silver balls.

DELICATELY SCENTED WITH ROSEWATER AND EACH
TOPPED WITH A SUGARED PETAL, THESE ELEGANT
CUPCAKES MAKE THE PERFECT TEATIME INDULGENCE
FOR MOM ON HER SPECIAL DAY.

Mother's Day

Preheat the oven to 350°F.

Beat the butter and sugar together in a bowl until pale and
fluffy, then beat in the eggs, one at a time. Sift the flour into
the mixture and fold in, then stir in the rosewater.

Spoon the mixture into the paper liners and bake in the
preheated oven for about 17 minutes until risen and golden
and a skewer inserted in the center comes out clean. Transfer
to a wire rack to cool.

To decorate, brush each rose petal with egg white and
sprinkle with superfine sugar. Leave to dry for about 1 hour.

Put 1½ tablespoons lemon juice in a bowl, then sift the
confectioner's sugar into the bowl and stir well. Add a little
more lemon juice as required to make a spoonable icing.
Add a few drops of food coloring to achieve a pale pink
icing, then spread over the cakes. Top each one with a
sugared rose petal. Leave to set before serving or packing.

1 stick unsalted butter,
at room temperature

½ cup granulated sugar

2 eggs

1 cup self-rising flour

1 tablespoon rosewater

TO DECORATE

12 pink rose petals, washed

1 egg white, beaten

1 tablespoon superfine sugar

1½–2 tablespoons freshly
squeezed lemon juice

1¼ cups confectioner's sugar

pink food coloring

*a 12-cup cupcake pan,
lined with paper liners*

MAKES 12

Father's Day

1 stick unsalted butter,
at room temperature

½ cup granulated sugar

2 eggs

1 cup self-rising flour

3 tablespoons unsweetened
cocoa powder

3 tablespoons full-fat milk

2 oz. white chocolate chips

1 cup mini-marshmallows

2 tablespoons slivered
almonds or brazil nuts

TO DECORATE

3½ oz. bittersweet chocolate,
finely chopped

½ cup heavy cream

3 tablespoons slivered
almonds or brazil nuts

¼ cup white chocolate chips

½ cup mini-marshmallows

*a 12-cup cupcake pan,
lined with paper liners*

MAKES 12

THE WINNING COMBINATION OF CHOC CHIPS, MINI MARSHMALLOWS, AND NUTS IN THESE "ROCKY ROAD" STYLE CUPCAKES IS GUARANTEED TO BE A HIT WITH DADS EVERYWHERE—ESPECIALLY THOSE WITH A SWEET TOOTH!

Preheat the oven to 350°F.

Beat the butter and sugar together in a bowl until pale and fluffy, then beat in the eggs, one at a time. Sift the flour and cocoa powder into the mixture and fold in. Stir in the milk, followed by the chocolate chips, marshmallows, and nuts.

Spoon the mixture into the paper liners and bake in the preheated oven for about 18 minutes until risen and the tops spring back when lightly pressed. Transfer to a wire rack to cool.

To decorate, put the chocolate in a heatproof bowl. Heat the cream in a saucepan until almost at a boil, then pour over the chocolate and leave to melt for about 5 minutes. Stir until smooth and creamy, then leave to cool for about 30 minutes until thick and glossy.

Spread the chocolate mixture over the cakes and stick the nuts, chocolate chips, and marshmallows into the frosting.

THESE ADORABLE FLOWER CAKES MAKE THE PERFECT
TREAT FOR GRANDPARENTS AND THE RECIPE IS EASY
ENOUGH FOR CHILDREN TO FOLLOW WITH SUPERVISION.
THEY'RE SO PRETTY NOBODY IN THE FAMILY WILL BE
ABLE TO RESIST STEALING ONE OR TWO!

Grandparent's Day

Preheat the oven to 350°F.

Beat the butter and sugar together in a bowl until pale and
fluffy, then beat in the eggs, one at a time. Sift the flour into
the mixture and fold in, then stir in the lemon peel.

Spoon the mixture into the paper liners and bake in the
preheated oven for about 18 minutes until risen and golden
and a skewer inserted in the center comes out clean. Transfer
to a wire rack to cool.

To decorate, put the confectioner's sugar and lemon juice in
a bowl and stir together until smooth and creamy. It should
be thick and spoonable, but not too runny. Divide the icing
among two bowls, add a few drops of food coloring to each
one, and stir well to make a good vibrant pink and blue.

Spoon the icing onto the cakes, allowing it to spread slightly
so that it resembles flower petals, then drop a sugar rosette
into the center of each flower. Let set before serving.

1 stick unsalted butter,
at room temperature

½ cup granulated sugar

2 eggs

1 cup self-rising flour

finely grated peel of 1 lemon

TO DECORATE

1 cup confectioner's sugar,
sifted

1–1½ tablespoons freshly
squeezed lemon juice

pink and blue food coloring

12 sugar rosettes

*a 12-cup cupcake pan,
lined with paper liners*

MAKES 12

½ cup granulated sugar

¼ teaspoon dried
lavender flowers

1 stick unsalted butter,
at room temperature

2 eggs

1 cup self-rising flour

2 tablespoons milk

TO DECORATE

1½ cups confectioner's sugar,
sifted

1 egg white

purple food coloring

12 small sprigs of
fresh lavender

*a 12-cup cupcake pan,
lined with paper liners*

MAKES 12

SUBTLY FLAVORED WITH LAVENDER FLOWERS, THESE
ELEGANT, GOLDEN CUPCAKES ARE DELICIOUS SERVED
MID-AFTERNOON WITH A NICE CUP OF TEA. THEIR
OLD-STYLE CHARM MAKES THEM THE PERFECT TREAT
FOR A MUCH-LOVED GRANDMA OR GREAT AUNT.

A Treat for Grandma

Preheat the oven to 350°F.

Put the sugar and lavender flowers in a food processor and
process briefly to combine. Tip the lavender sugar into a
bowl with the butter and beat together until pale and fluffy.

Beat the eggs into the butter mixture, one at a time, then
sift in the flour and fold in. Stir in the milk.

Spoon the cake mixture into the paper liners. Bake in the
preheated oven for about 18 minutes until risen and golden
and a skewer inserted in the center comes out clean. Transfer
to a wire rack to cool.

To decorate, gradually beat the confectioner's sugar into the
egg white in a bowl, then add a few drops of food coloring
and stir to achieve a pale lilac icing. Spoon the icing over
the cakes, then top each one with a sprig of fresh lavender.
Leave to set before serving.

A Surprise for Grandpa

DENSE AND ALMONDY WITH A STICKY MARZIPAN CENTER,
THESE CUPCAKES ARE REMINISCENT OF A TRADITIONAL
ENGLISH BAKEWELL TART. PACK A FEW IN A TIN AS A NICE
SURPRISE GIFT FOR A SWEET-TOOTHED GRANDPA OR
UNCLE AND WATCH THEM DISAPPEAR IN NO TIME.

Preheat the oven to 350°F.

Beat the butter and sugar together in a bowl until pale
and fluffy, then beat in the eggs, one at a time. Sift the
flour into the mixture and fold in, along with the ground
almonds and glacé cherries.

Spoon small dollops of the mixture into the paper cases,
sprinkle over some grated marzipan and top with the
remaining mixture. Bake in the preheated oven for about
18 minutes until risen and golden and a skewer inserted in
the center comes out clean. Transfer to a wire rack to cool.

To decorate, put the lemon juice and confectioner's sugar in
a bowl and stir until smooth and creamy. Spoon on top of
the cakes and top each one with half a glacé cherry. Leave
to set before serving or packing.

1 stick unsalted butter,
at room temperature

½ cup granulated sugar

2 eggs

scant ¾ cup self-rising flour

⅓ cup ground almonds

½ cup glacé cherries, halved

1 oz. marzipan, finely grated

TO DECORATE

2 tablespoons freshly
squeezed lemon juice

1⅜ cups confectioner's sugar,
sifted

6 glacé cherries, halved

*a 12-cup cupcake pan,
lined with paper liners*

MAKES 12

JUST FOR YOU!

Get Well Soon

LIGHT-AS-A-FEATHER GENOESE SPONGE TOPPED WITH
COOL CREAM AND NUTRITIOUS FRESH BERRIES MIGHT
BE JUST THE THING TO PERK UP A FRIEND WHO'S BEEN
FEELING UNDER THE WEATHER.

Preheat the oven to 350°F.

Put the eggs and sugar in a large bowl and beat for about
10 minutes until thick and pale. Add the vanilla extract.
Sift the flour into a separate bowl twice, then sift it into
the egg mixture and fold in.

Spoon the mixture into the paper liners and bake in the
preheated oven for about 12 minutes until risen and golden
and a skewer inserted in the center comes out clean. Transfer
to a wire rack to cool.

To decorate, whip the cream in a bowl until it stands in
peaks, then swirl over the cakes. Top with fresh berries,
dust with confectioner's sugar and serve immediately.

Note: As these cakes don't contain any fat they don't keep
well and are best eaten on the day they are made.

2 eggs

5 tablespoons granulated
sugar

1 teaspoon pure vanilla
extract

¾ cup all-purpose flour

TO DECORATE

⅔ cup heavy cream

1 pint fresh summer
berries, such as strawberries,
blueberries, raspberries,
and red currants

confectioner's sugar,
for dusting

*a 12-cup cupcake pan,
lined with paper liners*

MAKES 12

For a Great Teacher!

1 stick unsalted butter,
at room temperature

½ cup granulated sugar

2 eggs

1 cup self-rising flour

4 oz. dried apple rings,
finely chopped

TO DECORATE

2 oz. ready-to-roll
fondant icing

yellow, green and blue
food coloring

⅔ cup mascarpone

½ cup confectioner's sugar,
sifted

1 teaspoon fresh apple juice

*a 12-cup cupcake pan,
lined with paper liners*

mini-number cookie cutters

MAKES 12

WHAT BETTER WAY TO SAY THANK YOU TO A FAVORITE
TEACHER AT THE END OF TERM THAN TO BAKE UP
A BATCH OF THESE FUN APPLE-FLAVORED CUPCAKES.

Make the number decorations the day before you plan to
bake the cakes. Divide the fondant icing into two pieces.
Add a couple of drops of yellow food coloring to one
piece and green to the other and knead until the colors are
well blended. Roll out each piece between two sheets of
parchment paper or plastic wrap to ¼ inch thick. Stamp out
numbers using the cookie cutters. Leave to dry overnight.

Preheat the oven to 350°F.

Beat the butter and sugar together until pale and fluffy, then
beat in the eggs, one at a time. Sift the flour into the mixture
and fold in, then stir in the dried apple pieces.

Spoon the mixture into the paper liners and bake in the
preheated oven for 17 minutes until risen and golden and
a skewer inserted in the center comes out clean. Transfer
to a wire rack to cool.

To decorate, put the mascarpone, sugar, and apple juice in
a bowl and beat together until smooth. Add a few drops of
blue food coloring and mix well. Spread the frosting on top
of the cakes and stick the numbers into the frosting.

A Job Well Done

PACKED WITH COCONUT AND TANGY LIME, THESE
DELICIOUS CAKES WITH THEIR SNOWY-WHITE, RUFFLED
TOPS ARE EASY TO MAKE YET LOOK VERY IMPRESSIVE.
BAKE A BATCH AND OFFER THEM TO YOUR CO-WORKERS
TO ENJOY DURING THEIR COFFEE BREAK.

Preheat the oven to 350°F.

Beat the butter, coconut cream, and sugar together in a bowl
until pale and fluffy, then beat in the eggs, one at a time. Sift
the flour and baking powder into the mixture and fold in,
then stir in the coconut and lime peel, followed by the milk.

Spoon the mixture into the paper liners, then bake in the
preheated oven for about 17 minutes until risen and golden
and a skewer inserted in the center comes out clean. Transfer
to a wire rack to cool.

To decorate, beat the cream cheese, sugar, and lime juice
together in a bowl. Swirl the frosting on top of the cakes,
then sprinkle over the coconut shavings in a thick layer.

6 tablespoons unsalted butter,
at room temperature

2 tablespoons coconut cream

½ cup granulated sugar

2 eggs

¼ cup self-rising flour

1 teaspoon baking powder

3 tablespoons dried coconut

finely grated peel of 1 lime

2 tablespoons milk

TO DECORATE

5 oz. cream cheese

⅛ cup confectioner's sugar,
sifted

2 teaspoons freshly
squeezed lime juice

2 oz. moist coconut shavings

*a 12-cup cupcake pan,
lined with paper liners*

MAKES 12

½ cup soft brown sugar

⅔ cup sunflower oil

2 eggs

finely grated peel of 1 orange

seeds from 5 cardamom
pods, crushed

½ teaspoon ground ginger

1½ cups self-rising flour

2 small carrots
(about 5–6 oz.), grated

½ cup shelled walnuts
or pecans, roughly chopped

TO DECORATE

⅔ cup mascarpone

finely grated peel of 1 orange

1½ teaspoons freshly
squeezed lemon juice

⅓ cup confectioner's sugar,
sifted

*a 12-cup cupcake pan,
lined with paper liners*

MAKES 12

You're a Good Neighbor

LIGHTLY SPICED AND TOPPED WITH A CREAMY CITRUS
FROSTING, THESE TASTY CARROT CAKES ARE JUST THE
THING TO TAKE ROUND TO YOUR NEIGHBOR TO
SAY THANK YOU FOR ALWAYS BEING THERE TO LEND
A HELPING HAND.

Preheat the oven to 350°F.

Put the sugar in a bowl and break up using the back of a
fork, then beat in the oil and eggs. Stir in the orange peel,
crushed cardamom pods, and ginger, then sift the flour into
the mixture and fold in, followed by the carrot and nuts.

Spoon the cake mixture into the paper liners and bake in
the preheated oven for about 20 minutes until risen and
a skewer inserted in the center comes out clean. Transfer
to a wire rack to cool.

To decorate, beat the mascarpone, grated orange peel,
lemon juice, and sugar together in a bowl and spread the
frosting over the cakes.

THESE MARBLED CHOCOLATE CAKES WITH A FEATHERED
CREAM CHEESE AND CARAMEL FROSTING ARE SMART
AND INDULGENT. TAKE THEM TO FRIENDS NEXT TIME
YOU'RE INVITED TO DINNER AND ENJOY THEM AS DESSERT.

Thanks for Having Us

Preheat the oven to 350°F.

Beat the butter and sugar together in a bowl until pale and
fluffy, then beat in the eggs, one at a time. Sift the flour into
the mixture and fold in, then divide the mixture between
two bowls. Add the cocoa powder to one bowl and stir in.

Drop alternating teaspoonfuls of the two cake mixtures into
the paper liners. Using a skewer, cut through the mixture
a couple of times to marble it, then bake the cakes in the
preheated oven for 17 minutes until risen and golden and
a skewer inserted in the center comes out clean. Transfer
to a wire rack to cool.

To decorate, put the cream cheese and sugar in a bowl
and beat together until smooth and creamy, then stir in
the cream to make a smooth, creamy frosting. Spread the
frosting over the cakes, then drizzle or pipe lines of dulce
de leche over the top. Leave as they are, or draw a skewer
through the dulce de leche to give a feathered effect.

1 stick unsalted butter,
at room temperature

½ cup granulated sugar

2 eggs

1 cup self-rising flour

1 tablespoon unsweetened
cocoa powder

TO DECORATE

5 oz. cream cheese

⅓ cup confectioner's sugar,
sifted

2 tablespoons heavy cream

dulce de leche, for drizzling

*a 12-cup cupcake pan,
lined with paper liners*

MAKES 12

Index

Conversion chart

Weights and measures have been rounded up or down slightly to make measuring easier.

The recipes in this book require the following conversions:

American	Metric	Imperial
6 tbsp	85 g	3 oz
7 tbsp	100 g	3½ oz
1 stick	115 g	4 oz

Measuring butter:
A US stick of butter weighs 4 oz which is approximately 115 g or 8 tablespoons.

Volume equivalents:

American	Metric	Imperial
1 teaspoon	5 ml	
1 tablespoon	15 ml	
¼ cup	60 ml	2 fl oz
⅓ cup	75 ml	2½ fl oz
½ cup	125 ml	4 fl oz
⅔ cup	150 ml	5 fl oz (¼ pint)
¾ cup	175 ml	6 fl oz
1 cup	250 ml	8 fl oz

Weight equivalents:

Imperial	Metric
1 oz	30 g
2 oz	55 g
3 oz	85 g
3½ oz	100 g
4 oz	115 g
6 oz	175 g
8 oz (½ lb)	225 g
9 oz	250 g
10 oz	280 g
12 oz	350 g
13 oz	375 g
14 oz	400 g
15 oz	425 g
16 oz (1 lb)	450 g

Oven temperatures:

120°C	(250°F)	Gas ½
140°C	(275°F)	Gas 1
150°C	(300°F)	Gas 2
170°C	(325°F)	Gas 3
180°C	(350°F)	Gas 4
190°C	(375°F)	Gas 5
200°C	(400°F)	Gas 6
220°C	(425°F)	Gas 7

Measurements:

Inches	cm
¼ inch	5 mm
½ inch	1 cm
1 inch	2.5 cm
2 inches	5 cm
3 inches	7 cm
4 inches	10 cm
5 inches	12 cm
6 inches	15 cm
7 inches	18 cm
8 inches	20 cm
9 inches	23 cm
10 inches	25 cm
11 inches	28 cm
12 inches	30 cm